Michael A. Braun

Action against the pollution of the seas by oil

How was the international regime for protecting the oceans against the pollution from oil-tankers successful?

GRIN Verlag

Bibliografische Information der Deutschen Nationalbibliothek:

Die Deutsche Bibliothek verzeichnet diese Publikation in der Deutschen National-
bibliografie; detaillierte bibliografische Daten sind im Internet über http://dnb.d-
nb.de/ abrufbar.

Imprint:

Copyright © 2006 GRIN Verlag GmbH
Druck und Bindung: Books on Demand GmbH, Norderstedt Germany
ISBN: 978-3-640-19290-8

This book at GRIN:

http://www.grin.com/en/e-book/116896/action-against-the-pollution-of-the-seas-
by-oil

Hauptseminararbeit in the

Master of Arts in International Relations

Action against the pollution of the seas by oil

How was the international regime for protecting the oceans against the pollution from oil-tankers successful?

Hand in: Monday, November 27th, 2006

Word count: 6.280 (10.159) words on 19 (27) pages

Lehrstuhl für intl. Organisationen und intl. Politikfeldforschung

Wirtschafts- und sozialwissenschaftliche Fakultät der Uni Potsdam

Michael A. Braun, BA

Table of contents

Abstract

For a long time oceans were seen as vast and restless. In recent years, however, this view has changed since the pollution of the sea became an ever serious problem. Fairly cleaned liquids as well as various waste-pieces have massive implications on the maritime life. In addition, intentionally discharged as well as accidentally released oil-products propose a huge challenge to the global community.

Therefore the essay elaborates on this ecological issue with focus on oil-tankers as well as it lists up international actions taken against it. These are regime-induced (MARPOL 73/78) modifications at the ships itself such as load on top, segregated and protectively located ballast tanks, crude-oil-washing and double-hulls.

The hypothesis of the paper is that the international measures taken have been adequate in general and changed the discharging habits of the industry lastingly. The agreements also seem to have made it possible to have the oceans nowadays less polluted than it assumably would have been without them. Therefore, apart from minor potential future corrections, the international regime for protecting the oceans against the pollution from oil-tankers was rather successful.

Appendixes

List of references

Asendorpf (2006): Asendorpf, D., *Es läuft etwas schief aus See*, DIE ZEIT, Nr.37, p41, Hamburg 9/7/06

Backhaus (1992): Backhaus-Lautenschläger, C., *Ölwehr: Luftüberwachung verstärkt - Suchelektronik für Gewässerschutz*, Handelsblatt, Nr.92, pB4, Düsseldorf 5/13/92

Carpenter (2005): Carpenter, A., *The reduction of ship-generated waste in the North Sea: A contemporary analysis*, PhD thesis at the University of Leeds, Leeds 2005

COP (1996): Committee on oil pollution, *Effects of double-hull requirements on oil spill prevention*, National Academy Press, Washington 1996

Dahlmann (1994): Dahlmann, G. et al, Oiled seabirds – comparative investigations on oiled seabirds and oiled beaches in Denmark, the Netherlands and Germany 1990 - 1993, MARPOL Bulletin, vol.28, No.5, London, 1994

Fichtner (2003): Fichtner, U., *Die schwarze Front*, Der Spiegel, Nr.7, p58, Hamburg 2/10/03

Frey/Huelsmann (1993): Frey, P., / Huelsmann, A., *Mehr Sicherheit mit doppelter Hülle*, VDI Nachrichten, Nr.3, p4, Düsseldorf 1/22/93

Grosso (2006): Grosso, O., *Tödliches Treibgut der Konsumkultur*, Handelsblatt Nr.128, p9, Düsseldorf 7/6/06

Heumer (1999): Heumer, W., Das Risiko fährt immer mit: Mehr als jeder dritte Tanker weltweit gilt als überaltert und unsicher, VDI Nachrichten, Nr.51, p8, Düsseldorf 12/24/99

Heydemann (1992): Heydemann, B., Kiel will die kostenlose Entsorgung von Ölresten im Hafen nicht mehr fortführen, Handelsblatt, Nr.24, p4, Düsseldorf 2/4/92

Hollmann (2002): Hollmann, M., *Die Artenverschleppung über Ballastwasser ist ein bislang ungelöstes Problem*, VDI Nachrichten, Nr.3, p6, Düsseldorf 3/28/02

Holloway (1999): Holloway, M., *Oil in water*, Technology and Business - Environment, Scientific American, Vol.3/99, p39, New York 1999

Huijer (n.a.): Huijer, K., *Trends in oil spills from tanker ships 1995 – 2004*, Intl. Tanker Owners Pollution Federation, London [Internet 9/14/06] http://www. itopf.com/amop05.pdf

IMO (1978): Intl. Maritime Organisation, *International Convention for the Prevention of Pollution from Ships – modified by the Protocol of 1978 (MARPOL 73/78)*, London [Internet 9/9/06] http://www.imo.org/Safety/mainframe.asp?topic_id=258&doc_id=678#intro

IMO (1996): International Maritime Organisation, Focus on IMO: *Tanker safety – the work of the International Maritime Organisation*, IMO, London 1996

IMO (1998a): International Maritime Organisation, *Focus on IMO: MARPOL – 25 years*, IMO, London 1998

IMO (1998b): International Maritime Organisation, Focus on IMO: *Preventing Marine Pollution – The environmental threat*, IMO, London 1998

IMO (n.a.1): International Maritime Organisation, *IMO description of Crude-oil-washing*, London [Internet 9/9/06] http://www.imo.org/Environment/mainframe.asp?topic_id=306

IMO (n.a.2): International Maritime Organisation, *Tanker safety - preventing accidental pollution*, London [Internet 9/9/06] http://www.imo.org/Safety/index.asp?topic_id=155

ITOPF (n.a.): International Tanker Owners Pollution Federation Limited, *Trends in oil spills*, London [Internet 9/9/06] http://www.itopf.com/stats.html

Mitchell (1994): Mitchell, R., *International oil pollution at sea: environmental policy and treaty compliance*, Massachusetts Institute of Technology, Cambridge, MA, 1994

Morell (1997): Morell, Th., *Gefahr durch Öl in der Nordsee*, Der Tagesspiegel, Nr.16153, p40, Berlin 11/6/97

N.N. (1987a): N.N., *Nur magere Aussichten auf Fortschritte*, Handelsblatt, Nr.170, p6, Düsseldorf 9/7/87

N.N. (1987b): N.N., *Schmutziger Lorbeer*, Wirtschaftswoche, Nr.1, p66, Düsseldorf 1/2/87

N.N. (1990a): N.N., *Briten bestehen auf Verklappung*, Handelsblatt, Nr.31, p10, Düsseldorf 2/13/90

N.N. (1990b): N.N., *Umweltzerstörung durch Ölverschmutzung auf See ist nicht tragbar*, Handelsblatt, Nr.8, p20, Düsseldorf 1/11/90

N.N. (1999): N.N., *Im Öl-Tanker-Geschäft gelten nur wenige Sicherheitsnormen*, Der Tagesspiegel, Nr.16919, p24, Berlin 12/30/99

N.N. (2002): N.N., *Freispruch für Öltanker*, Der Spiegel, Nr.23, p163, Hamburg 6/3/02

Nelson (n.a.): Nelson, P., *Pollution from ships: A global perspective*, [Internet 9/14/06] http://www.aic.gov.au/publications/proceedings/26/nelson.pdf

Nixon (1998): Nixon, S.W., *The oceans: Enriching the sea to death*, Scientific American, p48-53, New York 1998

Peet (1994): Peet, G., *International co-operation to prevent oil-spills at sea: Not quite the success it should be*, in: Bergesen, H. / Parmann, G. (eds.), Green globe yearbook of international cooperation on environment and development, University Press, Oxford 1994

4

Scheerer (2000): Scheerer, M., *EU bleibt Konsequenzen aus jüngster Ölpest schuldig*, Handelsblatt, Nr.124, p12, Düsseldorf 6/30/00

Sesin (2000): Sesin, C.-P., *Der Kampf gegen Ölsünder zeigt erst wenig Wirkung*, Handelsblatt, Nr.49, p53, Düsseldorf 3/9/00

Smil (1997): Smil, V., *Global population and the nitrogen cycle*, Scientific American, p76-81, Vol.7/97, New York 1997

Strassmann (2002): Strassmann, B., Sauber auf See - Erstmals wird ein Schiff mit dem "Blauen Engel" ausgezeichnet, DIE ZEIT, Nr.47, p45, Hamburg 11/14/02

Tchobanoglos (2003): Tchobanoglos, G, et al, *Wastewater Engineering*, 4th ed., McGraw-Hill, New York City 2003

USCOP (n.a.): U.S. Commission on Ocean Policy, *Clear water ahead: Coastal and ocean water quality*, Washington [Internet 9/14/06] http://www.oceancommission.gov/documents/ prelimreport/ 05_clear_waters.pdf

West (2006): West, L., *A Billion People Worldwide Lack Safe Drinking Water*, [Internet 3/26/06] http://environment.about.com/od/environmentalevents/a/waterdayqa.htm

White / Baker (1998): White, I., / Baker, J., *The sea empress oil spill in context*, Paper for the conference on oil empress spill – Cardiff, 02/13/98, International Tanker Owners Pollution Federation, London [Internet 9/14/06] http://www.itopf.com/seeec.pdf

Willer (1988): Willer, K., *Zahlmeister gesucht*, Wirtschaftswoche, Nr.19, p127, Düsseldorf 5/6/88

Handout for the presentation in the seminar

23 November 2004 - Potsdam University

Seminar 'International regimes: Theory, empirics and policy'

Presenter: Michael A Braun, BA

Action against pollution of the sea – Regime induced innovation

Supervision of oil discharging by specific industrial requirements

Do you remember 24 March 1989? It was the day when super-tanker Exxon Valdez spilled about 35,000 tons of oil into Prince William Sound in Alaska. As probably most people you might think, such accidents are the main reason of oil pollution at sea. You are wrong! In fact they are not as far as bad as the normal discharges from usual operating tankers.

According to Mitchell tankers transported in 1953 some 250m tons of crude oil by sea and intentionally discharged some 300,000 of them. Yet 25 years later the growing volume of oil transported has increased the amount of discharged oil as well to some 5m tons a year (estimation). Over all this is responsible for about two third of ship-generated oil pollution. Only one third is because of accidents and of discharges that do not come from tankers.

But what is the reason for discharging oil? Image a bottle of milk. Once you have emptied it, there still is some white liquid at the walls - and that is the same with oil tankers. Once they have delivered their precious cargo, a small fraction still remains to the walls. Further on, as you want to use your bottle (or oil tanker) again you have to clean it. For this purpose two practises are widely used from the beginning since oil is transported by sea.

One is filling up the transportation tanks with seawater. The reason is not only cleaning but also as ballast to stabilize the empty ship while navigating to the next loading destination. The other one just means putting seawater with high pressure to the walls. Independent what method is used, both rinse the leftovers completely away – and into sea. Over all the oil-water-mixture (slops) represents only 0.3 to 0.5 % of total cargo – but you have to imagine the size of such super-tanker.

Therefore result is that oil pollution has got the longest history of international attraction.

1926: First international conference on oil pollution

1954: Intl. Convention for the Prevention of Pollution of the Sea by Oil (OILPOL)

1973: Intl. Convention for the Prevention of Pollution from Ships (MARPOL 73)

1978: Protocol to the MARPOL 73 (known together as MARPOL 73/78)

In the beginning (1926 & 1956) consultations were more or less some get together rather than outcome oriented. Compared to this MARPOL 73 – and later 78 - has lead to results. Over all lower reliance on humans at sea and a clear self-enforceable mechanism were the aims to be reached. Nevertheless at both there were debates from either ship-producing or ship-running countries. This becomes clear when talking about contents of the protocols.

To prevent the sea from further oil pollution caused by discharging, MARPOL 73/78 fixed two possible strategies: One is the method of segregated ballast tanks (SBT). This means tankers may have a separation of cargo, lines and slops inside. Obviously, this is preferred by ship-building countries since it involves higher turnover to their national shipyards. The other one is crude-oil-washing (COW). Idea is to reduce the waste of oil by dividing oil and sea-water before pumping the same back to sea. In this way it seems to be a cheap environmental alternative. This is preferred by ship-running countries and their ship-owners.

As a compromise the new requirements were put into practise as follows from 1979 onwards: SBT had to be built in ships that were produced newly afterwards; SBT or COW into the existing fleet. Therefore additional costs occurred for ship-owners that were not paid by the forcing governments nor someone else but by themselves. Over all these costs reeached from two to nine percent of the final price. Further on the – less time-intensive - maintenance of SBT is more expensive than COW. But this necessarily leads to the need of higher tonnage to make the same profits. Compared to this COW causes additional costs of only 1/3 of SBT – and is very attractive in oil crisis since it saves precious raw material.

From the more academic point of view this regime seems to be self-enforcing indeed. The reason is the cooperation of all actors involved. Since MARPOL 73/78 was a widely accepted protocol it became international law. Therefore ship-owners, ship-crews, oil companies and shipyards had to comply. Otherwise they would face massive problems with their own and foreign governments, port authorities and insurances.

In this way equipment standards simplify the task of monitoring compared to discharging standards greatly. For the global public it obviously is far easier to supervise just few big players as mentioned than some 7,000 tankers around the world (1984). Moreover the costs of this regime were in an economical sense quite low. Since it caused success (environment) and generated turnover, the additional cost to any litre of oil were little.

Used literature and websites:

Mitchell, Ronald. International oil pollution at sea: environmental policy and treaty compliance. Massachusetts Institute of Technology, Cambridge, MA, 1994

www.imo.org – International Maritime Organization (UN)

www.sciam.com – Scientific American magazine

1   Introduction and academic method

Water pollution at land as well as at sea is a serious problem in the global context. It has been suggested that it is worldwide the leading cause of death and disease.[1] Although natural phenomena (volcanoes, earthquakes etc.) also cause a decrease of quality, man-made water pollution is the biggest issue. This is easy to understand because humans accepted the oceans for a long time as vast and restless.

In these days liquid and substantial waste that came off land or was discharged at sea seemed to be just a 'drop into a giant, sloshing bucket'.[2] Nowadays scientists know this was wrong. Fairly cleaned liquids such as domestic sewage and industrial wastewater as well as wastepieces from household and industrial use have strong implications on the maritime life – and they lead back to the life at land.[3]

The sources of this accepted pollution are various. Sewage containing detergents, fertilizers and pesticides are spilt in. Hazardous outflows from construction sites and farms as well as acid rain round the menu.[4] But not only land-based, also sea-generated wastes from cruise- and cargo-ships challenge the oceans. Even intentionally (!) discharged oil[5]-products, which is nowadays not acceptable any more.

According to the question, the essay is focusing on action against the oil-pollution of the seas with respect to the one generated by oil-tankers. Of all ships, they account for the vast majority of oil due to their operational and accidental spills. However, one has to bear in mind that all cargo transport produces waste; and sea-transport is no exception. The crews, the handling and even the engines produce it. Therefore ships are not special apart from their size and area of operation.

But ocean ships were usually seen as environmentally friendlier.[6] Compared to the amount they carry, they only need a fraction of fuel. However, this does not take into account addi-

---

[1] Tchobanoglos (2003) – pp12: This statement was made especially for water-resources at land.
[2] Nixon (1998) – p51
[3] USCOP (n.a.) – pp155
[4] ibid / West (2006)
[5] Oil can refer to many different materials, including crude oil, refined petroleum products or its by-products as well as oily ballast water.
[6] Strassmann (2002)

tional polluting activities such as the release of oily liquids generated during operations, poisoning paint for the hull and the uncleaned exhausts.

Of these pollutions, oil-discharging is the most extensively studied one because it is estimated to contribute strongly to the decrease of the quality and cleanness of the marine environment. Furthermore it is the number one concern of the public, when it comes to the health of the oceans. This mourning, unfortunately, seems to come up only especially after major accidents. The continuing oil-pollution of the seas by indented releases is not known or not wanted to be seen. But a spill of any size can have massive effects, regardless its source or the area where it occurred.

For the essay, available data and literature in books, periodicals and industry-papers has been looked at from a sceptical perspective since all can only be estimations. In addition, a lot seems to have been launched or supported by lobbyists from either side. However, it is not surprising that research produces different results depending on affiliation. A useful indication is the findings anyway; whereas they do not provide an answer on the question, they still give indication.[7]

And a general trend can be detected – towards fewer intentional and accidental[8] oil-spills. In the same time this is also the hypothesis of the paper: The regime, the International Convention for the Prevention of Pollution from Ships[9] – known as MARPOL 73/78 – is able to regulate and eventually minimise ship-generated pollution of the seas when it comes to oil. So it is assumed the regime was successful.

To gain insight on the topic, the outline of the paper is as follows: a collection of ecological issues regarding maritime pollution will be presented after the introduction. This is followed by an elaboration on accidental and intended oil-discharging at sea. Later there is an introduction on the International Maritime Organisation, pre-MARPOL 73/78 agreements as well as the actual agreement and its amendments. At this point there will be also the four main re-

---

[7] In this context what is missing, is information about the extent of environmental damage caused by oil-spills. Of course this is available for areas in which accidents occurred. But what is with all the unnamed places that get contaminated every day by operational oil discharges from vessels?

[8] It is often stated that the number of (serious) tanker accidents went down dramatically as well as the amount of oil discharged. Therefore many consider MARPOL 73 / 78 to be very successful.

[9] IMO (1978)

gime-induced modifications at oil-tankers brought in. They are: load-on-top, the segregation and protective location of ballast tanks, crude-oil-washing and double-hulls. They will be explained en detail and their results are shown. This is followed by an assessment of the actions taken as well a brief conclusion, which finalizes the essay.

2 A deadly collection of ecological issues for the high seas

As outlined, high seas are contaminated in many ways.[10] The most often referred to are: marine debris, coastal water pollution, invasive species, vessel safety and vessel pollution. According to the topic, the essay will specify only on ship-[11]generated oil-discharging. But because all issues lead to the general deterioration of the water quality, they are listed up here for a better understanding.

The dumping of these (toxic) substances, usually plastic waste, happens from cruise ships[12] or by pouring in through rivers from the inner land as well as from coastal cities into the sea. So, experts estimate at least 300.000 pieces of plastics, the marine debris, swimming on each square kilometre of ocean-surface.[13] Plastic waste is seen as being able to 'survive' 100 years and more on oceans. In this time it erodes, but never completely disappears[14] and if animals eat it, it harms them.

But marine debris is more than plastic; it consists also of smoking leftovers, maritime activities (fishing, drilling) and even lost container cargo, that can be found some thousands of miles away from their origin. Experts estimate 80% of the total debris being washed off or blown in. The rest is seen as being discharged at sea.[15]

Another issue is nitrogen or phosphorous, which are essential ingredients of plant fertilizers.[16] Together with pesticides and heavy metals they are also washed away, in this case from farmland, and spilt at the coasts and into the high seas by rivers and rainfall. There the two substances fulfil their task nearly as good as at land – they grow organisms such as algae and contribute to the change of balance.

---

[10] Strassmann (2002) – This goes with a massive pollution of the maritime air. Large ships release with the exhaust huge amounts of harmful substances. One number: Within harbour cities, that accounts for up to 80% of the total air pollution – including traffic and industrial activity.

[11] Ships pollute oceans in many ways: oil-spills and dioxide from exhausts, noise that disturbs the wildlife, and the water from ballast tanks that spreads harmful algae and invasive species.

[12] Grosso (2006) – Though ships have to dispose waste properly by law, some still do not care, but discharge their various wastes right away at sea.

[13] ibid – This could be things like old fishing nets, plastic bottles and shopping bags.

[14] ibid – Experts found, that plastic parts tend to shrink and break. Nevertheless, little pieces, so called micro plastics with less than 0,3 mm size, still remain in the oceans life circle.

[15] USCOP (n.a.) – pp211

[16] Nixon (1998) – The growing world population consumes an ever larger amount of these materials. Its factor doubled only between 1950 and 1985 due to more people and a protein-richer diet.

Luckily, in recent years developed countries used wastewater-treatment to a larger extend. Also developing countries realised the importance of such technologies – and acknowledge the fact, that the main issue is the ongoing growth of their populations.[17]

Another, less obvious, but very important polluter is the migration of invasive species.[18] This means that non-native maritime species travel from one to another place in the vast ballast waters of ocean going ships.[19] They carry this to stabilize their travel in times of low or no load. It is estimated that constantly about 7,000 different species are 'travelling' around the world on the oceans as a blind passenger.[20] And, unlike other forms of pollution that diminish over time, successful invasive species persist, increase and spread in new surroundings.

Finally, obvious challenges are liquids other than residues of plant fertilizers that are disposed intentionally or accidental without clearing them before releasing.[21] The worst water pollution, however, is possibly the release of mineral oil and its by-products.[22] It is able to damage easily immense parts of the maritime flora and fauna substantially and sustainable. The environmental effects of spilt oil vary depending upon the type and amount of the material spilt. Although it is technically all natural, its certain toxic substances do harm all creatures of the seas.

In general, lighter refined petroleum products such as diesel and gasoline are more likely to mix with water and are more toxic to marine life, but tend to evaporate relatively quick and do not stay long in the environment. Heavier crude oil, while of less immediate toxicity, can remain on the water or at the coast much longer.[23]

Researcher found that oil that is spilt for whatever reason, influences sea life massively not only for ten, but for dozens of years.[24] It even affects the DNA and therefore changes nature in a permanent way. And since many toxins decompose to tiny particles which are taken up e.g.

---

[17] Smil (1997) pp76 - Since leading experts assume another doubling of the release of nitrogen and phosphorous within the next 25 years, there seems to be no way than lowering the levels of waste spill into the seas.
[18] Asendorpf (2006) – p41
[19] USCOP (n.a.) – pp199
[20] ibid – p203
[21] West (2006) – Most water pollutants are eventually carried by rivers into the sea. Each step up the food chain concentrates the toxins e.g. heavy metals and pesticides by approx. the factor of ten.
[22] IMO (1998b)
[23] Fichtner (2003) – In the *Erika* event, oil split up into pieces of the size of coins; deadly for birds.
[24] Holloway (1999) – p39

by plankton, they concentrate and enrich upwards within the food chain and the results directly go back to men sooner or later[25]. Because most animal feeds contain fish oil and fish flour, toxins can be found not only in fish but also in land-based food such as meat, eggs and milk.

But why is it, if oil-spills have those enormous implications on the maritime eco-system,[26] released anyway? Vessels for example give oil way for various reasons, including accidental spills, during regular engine operation and indented discharging of waste-liquids to get cheaply rid of them. This especially applies in times of high fuel prices when many ship-owners use the cheap but environmentally dirty heavy oil to run their engines – which often leads also to more intended discharge of the leftovers.[27] Therefore discharge is also a false understanding of business to try to operate ships at the lowest possible point of costs, maintenance and time.[28]

However, with the development of inspection regimes, it has become easier to identify incidents of pollution. Although there are thousands of tankers shipping oil-products around the world, new technologies make this more possible. Although, unless a vessel can be directly linked with a specific spill, e.g. because another ship-crew or an air surveillance team can proof it, it is still not possible to blame the owner and claim the cost for cleaning up. But there is hope from another direction: Many of the ships were built in the 1970s and had to be modified in recent years due to international regulations – and so became safer.

In this chapter, the latter will be discussed more in depth and fundamentals will be given to evaluate the measures that have been taken to change this practice.

2.1 Accidents and unintended actions

The highly memorable crash of super-tanker *Exxon Valdez* in March '89 into the Alaskan Prince William Sound is one example of huge ocean pollution.[29] About 35,000 tons of oil flow in an area that formerly was untouched nature, both under and above water. After that day,

---

[25] Apart from sea birds, which are considered to be most likely to die instantly after getting in contact with oil, also oyster-, salmon- and other fish- and seafood-farms are heavily affected.
[26] Holloway (1999) – p39
[27] Willer (1988)
[28] Peet (1994) – p43
[29] White / Baker (1998) – Compared to the biggest oil-spill ever, which was about 270.000 tons, from a tanker crash off Trinidad and Tobago in 1979, this is not worth more than a foot note.

however, life was different for all local creatures. And even in the US-capital it led to remarkable changes in both, the (US) public perception on oil-pollution as well as a change of US-federal law on oil-spills.[30]

In Europe, a couple of accidents happened in the last decades with influence on nature and public opinion. In 1998 *Pallas* stranded off Germany and one year later *Erika* crashed off France. The worst Europe has seen so far, however, happened in 2002 in Spain when *Prestige* broke and spilt huge amounts of the dirty heavy oil.[31]

But not only groundings and collisions with rocks or man-build installations account for unintended oil-spills, also crashes with other tankers raise the numbers.[32] And sometimes even explosions or creep material tiredness get ships vulnerable and cause a break. Despite this, the numbers show: by amount most accidental spills result rather from accidents, but routine operations (e.g. loading) in ports.

In general, one sees crews usually are not trained well enough and lack confidence in critical situations. In most cases the pollution seems to be the result of insufficient technical conditions, lacking maintenance and the latter mentioned training.

Therefore accidents and unintended oil-releases are a strong reason for the pollution of coasts and oceans.[33] Also drilling platforms near the coast, land-based refineries near the sea, contaminated rivers and even natural seeping of oil directly from the source[34], account for it.[35] Nevertheless, as one might think, the mentioned factors are NOT the main reason of oil-pollution.[36] Estimations go as far as only 5 to 33% of all oil discharged comes from accidents.

---

[30] Scheerer (2000) / USCOP (n.a.)

[31] Fichtner (2003) / Strassmann (2002) – Heavy oil is the leftover of refineries. It only can be used as poisoning and dirty fuel for ships and power plants. The latter mainly applies for emerging countries, whereas 90% of all tanker- and container-ships use it. Its unbeatable price of only 50% of Diesel makes ship-owners forget they turn their ships into burning plants for hazardous waste.

[32] ITOPF (n.a.)

[33] ibid – Estimations assume a ton lost every million tons shipped at sea. Nevertheless, there is also a massive environmental issue related with the land-based transport of oil in pipelines.

[34] N.N. (2002) – Estimation states that over 170m litres of oil are spilled into the oceans every year. Also, one has to mention that oil is released from natural geologic dwells on the seafloor.

[35] Not to mention actions taken during wars. It is estimated that the 1983 Iranian-Iraqi war and the 1991 Golf war spilled 30 times more oil into the Persian Golf than Exxon Valdez did in Alaska.

[36] Peet (1994) – p42

[37] But what is the malus instead? The rest results from oil-contaminated ballast water and cleaning water...

2.2 Intended oil-discharging on sea

So, again, what is the reason for discharging oil at sea? For a better understanding one can imagine a bottle of milk. Once it is emptied, there still is some white liquid at the walls - and that is the same with oil-tankers. Once they have delivered their cargo, a fraction still remains to the walls. Further on, as one wants to use the bottle (or oil-tanker) again, one has to clean it. For this purpose two practises are widely used from the beginning since oil is transported by sea.

One is filling up the tanks (partly) with seawater. The reason is not only cleaning, but also as ballast to stabilize the empty ship while navigating to the next loading destination. The other is splashing seawater with high pressure to the walls. Independent what purpose it is for, both rinse leftovers away – into sea.[38] The total oil-water-mixture (slops) is only 0.3 to 0.5 % of the cargo – but the size of a tanker …

Tankers transported in 1953 some 250m tons of oil and intentionally discharged some 0,3m of them[39]. Yet 25 years later the transport-volume has increased; by that time the discharged oil was some 5m tons a year with projected increase. This practise has lead to a permanent pollution of beaches and a change in the maritime fauna and flora all over the world. For this, experts estimate[40] that 2/3 of the birds that died of oily substances did so by the intended discharge of unusable leftovers within the engine. Another 1/5 did so by the intended discharge of slops.

In the past oil slicks were splashed with chemicals to prevent them from reaching the coast.[41] Unfortunately experience showed that the chemicals or the combinations they form with the oil could be more harmful than the oil itself. So, nowadays released oil is tried to be caught right at sea. Only in the case of the immediate danger that the oil is blown towards coasts, ex-

---

[37] N.N. (2002)
[38] Morell (1997) – The '99 MARPOL amendment asked to include the cost of separating and cleaning the slops into the harbour fees. With this there would be less incentive to discharge at sea.
[39] Mitchell (1994)
[40] Morell (1997)
[41] Tchobanoglos (2003)

perts still use chemicals. And if too late, practise is to take the oily sands away rather than use chemicals as well.

There is also the issue of operational oil-pollution, both legal and illegal. All ships do discharge oily substances, which are generated in the engine room and also can enter in the bilges of the vessels, during their operational lifetime. Certain legal discharges are allowed according to international agreements and occur during normal operations in designated areas. Illegal, however, is the discharge of more than the agreed level of oil as well as in restricted areas such as the North Sea.[42]

---

[42] Morell (1997) – In 1997 the North Sea became such a "Particularly Sensitive Sea Area". Same applies for the Baltic, the Mediterranean, the Red and the Dead Sea as well.

3   International Maritime Organisation, or the arise of a regime

According to the paper's hypothesis the relative pollution per delivered unit has decreased[43] due to technical improvements as to be argued. This happened despite the fact that the amount of oil globally transported massively increased. This success, however, might not have taken place if a major UN resolution was not made in 1948. At this time, the London based inter-governmental Maritime Consultative Organisation was approved to be erected.[44] With this the shipping- and oil industry have undergone a transformation from self-regulating to a more regulated sector.

The organizations main task was to make shipping of all types, including tankers, safer. The measures in conventions and recommendations apply to these as well as other ships – and the safer a ship is, the less likely it is to cause an accident.[45] Moreover their task was to work against the pollution of the oceans and a better dealing with the issue of oil-discharging.[46] Additional duties are to strengthen the cooperations in shipping and standards of security and navigation. In 1982 they skipped 'consultative' and changed to International Maritime Organisation.[47]

By now, the International Maritime Organisation supported the issue of some very influential agreements on a global basis against oil-pollution such as MARPOL 73/78. And since oil is supposed to have the most substantial environmental implications to the seas, it also has the longest[48] and strongest[49] history of international environmental attention, which will be presented briefly in the following.

---

[43] ITOPF (n.a.) – Within the last 30 years oil-spills from tanker ships decreased massively. Compared to the 1970s, the 1980s and 1990s were estimated to have spilled only for 1/3 into the oceans; whereas the new century so far only accounts for 1/2 of the latter decade …
[44] Although the convention was ready for signature, their actual operation happened only in 1958 due to the massive influence of the shipping industry on the 'Consultative Organisation'.
[45] IMO (n.a.2)
[46] IMO (1998b) – In general, the IMO aims to prevent operational pollution, reduce accidents as well as their consequences, provide compensation and help with the implementation of its law.
[47] Membership varies by now at about 125 states.
[48] N.N. (1987b) – Over a dozen international agreements work on the issue of maritime pollution; and most of them were signed only in the last 40 years.
[49] Peet (1994) – p41

3.1   Pre-MARPOL 73/78 agreements

Since the aftermaths of the World War I era, maritime oil-pollution was sent on the agenda and recognised as an issue to the international and especially the US and British politics.[50] Following two different national regulations, also from the US and the UK, in 1926 the first International Conference on Oil-pollution was held in Washington DC. At this venue the participating countries were able to sign a treaty, which included the definition of what is the 'purity of the sea-water' as well as it was decided at which places the discharge of oil was allowed.

But it took till 1954 to gather for another meeting, the International Convention for the Prevention of Pollution of the Sea by Oil (OILPOL). Although its outcome was still limited like in 1926 in comparison to later regulations, the topic was brought up again and never went off the agenda from than.[51] This has possibly something to do with the skyrocketed western demand for middle-eastern crude oil after World War II; and so did the need for tanker-cleaning and other operations increase – resulting in ever more oil-discharge as well as accidents.

When the topic was discussed in 1926 and 1954, consultations were more like a nice get-together than outcome-oriented.[52] In 1972[53], however, the International Regulations for the Prevention of Collisions at Sea (COLREGS) was the first convention to contain special requirements for ships such as tankers which had reduced ability to manoeuvre. Also amendments to the '54-convention came up to reduce the amount of oil spilt rather than just to redistribute it. In addition, the 1974 International Convention for the Safety of Life at Sea (SOLAS) made ships safer and seas more clean. Despite this there were still some massive incidents and many of these were citied to human errors as main factors[54] – which made it more necessary to reach for a global and valid agreement on that topic.

---

[50] Before this, only some harbours faced environmental issues of oil; crude oil was not common.
[51] IMO (1996)
[52] Mitchell (1994) – pp85; Of course, especially the British would see it not this way, but serious.
[53] N.N. (1990b) – In between, however, there have been different initiatives on the topic such as the one 1958 in Geneva, the one 1969 on *Torrey Canyon* and the one from 1971. This introduced the Tanker Owners Voluntary Agreement Concerning Liability for Oil Pollution as well as the Contract Regarding an International Supplement to Tanker Liability for Oil Pollution.
[54] To cope with these errors, the International Management Code for the Safety of Ships and for Pollution Prevention, a guideline to ship-owners for their ships and their organisations, was made.

3.2 The MARPOL 73/78 agreement and its amendments

So, in 1973 the first general – in terms of being responsible for all kinds of maritime pollution – International Convention for the Prevention of Pollution from Ships (MARPOL 73) was planned and seen to be an update of the latter convention. It was extensively discussed and became signed, but never went into force for various reasons. One is simply that the participating parties were not able to find common ground on how to introduce it. Only one year later, however, SOLAS redefined parts of MARPOL 73 in special requirements for tankers.[55]

The true and final ratification of most other parts of MARPOL 73 happened after ongoing discussions in 1978 with the Protocol to MARPOL 73. It entered into force in October 1983. Today the package is mostly referred to as MARPOL 73/78[56] but is also known as Ship Pollution protocol in general. Compared to other agreements, especially the ones of 1926 and 1956, MARPOL 73/78 has lead to measurable results and was modified by many amendments over the years.

It was designed to minimise the pollution of the seas at sea, including dumping, oil-discharge and exhaust pollution. The superior object was to preserve the marine environment through the elimination of pollution by oily substances, mixtures and other harmful substances as well as the minimization of accidental outflows of such substances.[57] It also asks harbour cities to provide possibilities to dump ballast water and other waste waters properly.[58] And finally it pushes responsible ship-owners to change their internal policies in terms of better technical standards.

In addition to this, especially the American Oil-pollution Act of 1990 had a great influence on the US and international maritime shipping scene[59] and fired back and forth at many

---

[55] IMO (n.a.2) – E.g., fire safety rules became stricter for tankers than for ordinary dry-cargo ships.

[56] For an easy remember one decided to short 'marine pollution' and the years 1973 and 1978.

[57] N.N. (1990a) – One example would be that Britain fought till 1992 against a general dumping stop of liquids into the North Sea. They did not see any reason not to discharge industrial sewage, whereas Germany, Denmark and many other MARPOL signers did.

[58] N.N. (1987a) – While the absence of adequate reception facilities in some harbours does not justify illegal discharging of oil, it makes compliance with the rules not really easier. To encourage ship companies to follow the MARPOL agreements more strictly, some German harbours provided 1988 to 1990, with federal monies, the free of charge disposal of liquids at their premises.

[59] ITOPF (n.a.)

MARPOL 73 / 78 amendments as well.[60] This is also why the regime got a number of amendments to respond on changes in technology, knowledge and economic issues. So, since 1978 a series of annexes (I - V) and amendments (21) has modified the regulations.[61] The amendments are widely seen a necessary, although they often only have arisen after another major incident.[62]

---

[60] COP (1996) pp preface v / pp3 - This act was also to minimize the effects of oil-spills. Under the impressions of *Exxon Valdez* in 1989 it caused massive law changes demanded by the US congress and got quickly introduced. These were e.g. the unconditional rule of having double-hulls in US waters. For a 25-year period the phase-out of single-hull ships was allowed and an operational makeup of shipping companies was asked by law.

[61] Annex I is on regulations for the prevention of pollution by oil. Annex II is on regulations for the control of pollution by noxious liquid substances in bulk. Annex III is on regulations for the prevention of pollution by harmful substances carried by sea in packaged form or in freight containers, portable tanks or road and rail wagons. Annex IV is on regulations for the prevention of pollution by sewage from ships. Annex V is on regulations for the prevention of pollution by garbage from ships.

[62] Fichtner (2003) – Same applies for the EU: There were also some tanker accidents that caused massive oil pollution. Nevertheless, France e.g. does not do the needed number (25%) of random ship checks, but only one in ten; therefore EU law has partly failed.

4   Regime-induced modifications and procedures at oil-tankers

According to the International Maritime Organisation more reliance on humans at sea and a clear self-enforceable mechanism were the aims to be reached. Nevertheless at both were debates put from ship-producing and ship-running countries. Therefore there was a clear need for widely agreed action against the oil-pollution at sea. This becomes clear when talking about the specific behaviour of oil at sea.

Oil, which got into the oceans, is decomposed through physical, chemical and biological processes.[63] In the beginning (1) the oil spreads over the water surface and (2) the oil slick breaks into smaller parts. And within (3) 24 hours the misting parts evaporate. Light crude oil e.g. can diminish to only 50% of the original amount within half a day. The heavier parts remain in the water[64], are processed and dissolved by bacteria and other micro organisms. At sea the oil-pollution is mainly a danger to birds but also mammals and reptiles.[65] The bird's plumage is instantly damaged and as they are trying to clean it, they just poison themselves.[66]

To prevent the nature from this a compromise for good, for environmentalists as well as oil and shipping lobbyists, including requirements was put into practise as follows from 1979 respectively 1982[67]: protectively located segregated ballast tanks had to be built into ships that were produced newly. For the existing fleet there was a choice of either going for the segregation of ballast tanks or for crude-oil-washing. Therefore, in any case, additional costs occurred for ship-owners that were not paid by the forcing governments nor someone else but by themselves. In total, these costs reached from about two to nine percent of the final ship price.[68]

Moreover, the – although less time-intensive – maintenance of segregated ballast tanks is expensiver than the process of crude-oil-washing. But this necessarily leads to the need for a higher tonnage to make at least the same profits. Compared to this, crude-oil-washing causes additional costs of only 1/3 compared to segregated ballast tanks[69] – and is very attractive in oil-crisis since it saves precious raw material. In addition, especially for oil-tankers another

---

[63] N.N. (1990b)
[64] Depending on weather, wind and strength of waves sometimes a lotion of water and oil builds.
[65] Dahlmann (1994)
[66] Fichtner (2003)
[67] Before this, the idea of load-on-top was introduced already.
[68] Mitchell (1994)
[69] Mitchell (1994)

must-have was asked for introduction later as described in the following: double-hulls compared to single-hulls to protect the hazardous freight against accidental spills into the sea.

In addition to the technical measures (double-hulls, ballast tanks and crude-oil-washing) as discussed in the following, several 'weak' factors also account for less oil-pollution at sea. These are: specific ship management requirements such as the International Safety Management Code, adequate crew licensing certification and training requirements as well as stronger port controls and inspections.

From an academic point of view the regime is self-enforcing indeed. The reason is the intended / unintended (technical) cooperation of all actors involved. Since MARPOL 73/78 finally became a widely accepted protocol in terms of governments, it became also international law. Therefore other actors as ship-owners and crews, oil companies and shipyards had to just comply. Otherwise they face issues with their own and foreign governments, port authorities and insurances in terms of penalties, fees and denied entrance. Bearing this in mind, the regime for all tankers became successful by involving only this few 'key players'.[70]

4.1 Load-on-top technique

When oil is unloaded at the final destination there remains still some fraction of it at the walls of the tanks (like milk). The common procedure was to rinse the oil with seawater-jets off and pump it overboard into the sea.[71] This led to a considerable amount of oil getting into the sea and was not good for the cargo owner since precious oil is left in the tanks. The 1954 OILPOL Convention attempted to reduce the harm by prohibiting such discharges within 50 miles of most land and 100 miles of certain sensitive areas. Therefore in 1962 three oil companies[72] announced the new and technically important idea of a load-on-top system.

---

[70] N.N. (1987b) / Backhaus (1992) – To find out if an actor is cheating MARPOL 73/78 (intentional oil-discharges without permission) there is even more ways. The German federal government e.g. as well as some states, provide a screening based on laser waves and aircrafts. It performs its work either from ships or from airplanes and detects not only oil, but also many other hazardous liquids such as chemicals in the water.

[71] IMO (1998b)
[72] Shell, ESSO and British Petroleum

This allowed tanker crews to clean the tanks as previously using seawater. However, instead of pumping the resulting mixture overboard, it is pumped into a special slop tank.[73] During the journey the lighter oil will go up whereas the heavier water will sink down from where it is released to the sea. This however will need a well trained crew to make sure not to discharge more liquid than just the water.[74]

The process had advantages for the oil owner, since the oil normally lost during cleaning could be saved, but the main beneficiary was the environment. And clearly, observers argue without this system the pollution of the seas would have reached new heights in the last decades. Some experts believe that without load-on-top the amount of oil being dumped into the sea as a result of tank cleaning could have reached more than 8 million tons a year. Nevertheless, load-on-top is not yet the ideal way to go. Therefore the concept of segregated ballast tanks was developed to eliminate at least one source of pollution as described as follows.

4.2   Segregation and protective location of ballast tanks

In terms of the pollution of the seas by oil there is also an issue linked with ballast tanks: some ships do not even have large enough ones. Once the ship is completely empty, the crew just fills the original cargo tanks – containing usually oil – with seawater. With this they are able to create additional ballast tank space as well as they can clean the tanks from unwanted oily leftovers of former cargo. Due to this oceans have to cope with thousands of tons of oil-water mixtures.[75]

To protect the environment against such behaviour the International Maritime Organisation has introduced another MARPOL 73/78 amendment. This asks for the separation of ballast and cargo tanks as mentioned or, at least, the purchase of equipment to separate the oil-water mixture prior to releasing into the oceans. In addition computers monitor and report how much of each liquid is spilt.

This measure has two aspects to prevent unnecessary oil-discharging: (1) ballast water does not have to be contaminated by oil at all and so removes the problem of discharging it. This

---

[73] By the way: Same applies for ballasting, the process of taking up ballast water.
[74] IMO (1998b) – Estimations go as far as 800 tons of oil saved by every load of a large tanker.
[75] Heydemann (1992) – In the free-of-charge time between June '88 and May '91 400.000 tons of oil-mixtures were disposed in German harbours, which otherwise may have ended in the sea.

means that there is a need for separate ballast tanks, which are only loaded sometimes with ballast seawater. This means also, that oil-tankers have to have a separation of cargo, lines and slops inside.[76] Obviously, this technique always was preferred by ship-building countries since it involves additional / higher turnover to their national shipyards. But (2) the tanks are also positioned where the impact of a collision or grounding is likely to be greatest. In this way the amount of cargo spilt after an accident will be greatly reduced. In addition to this, the MARPOL-amendments of 1983 bans the transportation of oil in front tanks, which are the ship's most vulnerable points in the event of a collision.

So, a ballast tank has to be a separate compartment that holds seawater. Decades ago this was not the case, but cargo and ballast tanks were the same. Nowadays ships may have a ballast tank near the centre or multiple ones on either side.[77] Such can be filled or emptied to adjust the needed amount of force. However, big ships must take on ballast always for stability; even when travelling with cargo.[78]

The procedure of ballast water itself however can lead to the issue of invasive species.[79] Since ballast water taken from one part of the world and released in another one can introduce foreign aquatic life. This discharge has been responsible for the introduction of species that cause environmental and economic damage.[80]

4.3 Crude-oil-washing

A more recent possibility for tanker-crews to rinse remaining oil from the walls, compared to load-on-top, is the concept of crude-oil-washing. This is to reduce the waste of oil by using oil

---

[76] Mitchell (1994)

[77] IMO (1998b)

[78] COP (1996) pp41 – The location of ballast tanks, cargo tanks and other structures built in can be designed independently to suit the owner's requirements. Only demands of the classification society, flag state regulations and other regulations have to be met. These decisions, however, affect a range of factors such as capacity and costs and during the design process many trade-offs have to be made. Also the MARPOL demands for a location at the very bottom of the ship have to be met.

[79] Hollmann (2002) – Large cargo ships need ballast tanks to stabilized themselves. Even with no freight aboard, they still need to have about 30% load only from ballast water – including sea life.

[80] One example is the zebra mussel in the Great Lakes of North America. To prevent this the International Maritime Organisation suggests ship-owners to load and unload ballast water only at the wide ocean with a depth of more than 2,000 meters.

instead of seawater.[81] This seems to be a cheap and environmentally friendly alternative. It is preferred by ship-running countries and their ship-owners because it involves less investment and saves crude oil.[82] However, this MARPOL 73 / 78 concept only works with effort of the ship-owner. And since the International Maritime Organisation members know this, they have put the 1978 International Convention on Standards of Training, Certification and Watch keeping for Seafarers into practise, which is aimed of workers on tankers.

Starting in the 1970s, equipment capable of using oil itself for washing began to replace the water-based washing, leading to crude-oil-washing.[83] This technique means rinsing out the residue from the walls of an oil-tanker by using the cargo itself. When sprayed onto the sediments at the tank walls, the oil dissolved them, turned them back to usable oil that could be pumped off with the rest of the cargo. There is no need for slop tanks since the process leaves virtually no slops.

Crude-oil-washing makes the cleaning more effective than water[84] and allows the oil to be recovered and sold. It increases the amount of cargo discharged[85] and provides a further benefit to the cargo owner. It therefore ideally replaces the seawater washing systems of load-on-top, which always involved discharging some slops into the sea.[86] So, the system helps to prevent further ocean pollution from operational measures and is mandatory on new tankers under MARPOL 73/78.[87]

4.4 Single-hull turned into double-hull tankers

About one and a half years after the *Exxon Valdez* incident the US Oil-pollution Act 1990 was signed, mainly introducing the need for newly built ships to have a double-hull in order to stop in a US harbour.[88] The core of this is to reduce the probability of an oil-spill into the sea by 90%. Also an amendment to MARPOL 73/78 made it 1992 globally mandatory for oil-tankers of a bigger size and ordered after July 1993 to come with double-hulls. This require-

---

[81] N.N. (1987b) – Although MARPOL 73/78 seems to be environmentally friendly, it still allowed for a time a regulated discharge of oil into the sea from points at least 12 miles away off the coasts.
[82] Nelson (n.a.)
[83] IMO (1998b) – pp3
[84] ibid
[85] ibid
[86] Crude-oil-washing was made mandatory with MARPOL 73/78.
[87] IMO (n.a.1)
[88] Frey (1993)

ment has also been applied to existing ships[89] from 1995 on. All tankers that carry oil have to be converted or taken out of service when they reach an age of up to 30 years. Especially the second rule, however, was stretched over years because the capacity of shipyards is limited and it is impossible to convert all single-hull tankers to double-hulls without causing a disruption to world trade and the industry.

Following the *Erika* incident off the coast of France in 1999,[90] the member states of the International Maritime Organisation discussed an even stricter timetable for the phasing-out of single-hull tankers,[91] which entered into force in September 2003. Later new regulations on the prevention of oil-pollution from oil-tankers were made for the case when carrying heavy grade oil. Now the carriage of this is banned in medium and big single-hull tankers after April 2005, and in small ones after 2008. Also the final phasing-out date is brought forward to 2010, from 2015.

Before double-hulls were introduced the protective location of segregated ballast tanks was demanded. But since oil-tankers do not need ballast tanks all around their hull, there was always a severe chance for getting hurt at an area which was not protected by a ballast tank. Therefore the double-hull system came to succeed that gambling which two famous examples for single-hull accidents and accidental oil-spills played: the *Erika* and *Prestige*. Both were quite old and technically not most advanced. They were produced in Japan in mass-production in the late 1970s and had only the minimum thickness of steel. A double-hull ship instead assumably should have kept the load inside in case of such non-severe incidents.

Also, the space between outer and inner hull could be used a space for ballast water.[92] However, critics argue that the two to three meters between the two hulls are not enough to save the ship in an event that happens with high speed.[93]

However, a tanker with all this security equipment cannot be operated such as an ordinary ship – personnel has to be trained specifically[94] and be aware of its responsibility. And since a

---

[89] Heumer (1999) – I.e. they get an additional hull inside their existing walls; this means their loading capacity will be reduced by up top 30%.
[90] Investigations by the French government and the Maltese maritime authority concluded that age, corrosion and insufficient maintenance were contributing to the structural failure of the ship.
[91] Scheerer (2000)
[92] IMO (1998b)
[93] ibid

ship-crew usually comprises of many different nationalities and levels of education the International Safety and Management Code was introduced to get them on the same knowledge base. Experts estimate that for about 80% of all accidents human misbehaviour can be accounted. Therefore even the technology cannot help, but the people.[95]

Although the idea of double-hull tankers is generally seen as a great step forward, there still is doubt about its use. Double-hulls are mandatory from 2015 onwards – but to please the oil and cargo industry there is exceptions: So, states are allowed to licence single-hull ships till than as well for another 25 years.[96] This exception has caused critics to state that MARPOL 73/78 is more in favour of the industry (oil giants, ship-owners and emerging markets) than the nature.[97] By now yet at least a fifth of all ships worldwide are seen as being out of date. Longer phase-out dates or a state-depended prolongation are not the way to please the environment.

4.5 Assessment of the actions taken – and ideas beyond

The prevention of oil-spills is a massive undertaking, which involves decision makers at various levels. Key-actors were addressed with success; but future prevention-efforts focus on individuals. Also according to the latter description as well as this paper in general, the actions that have been taken were various in their kind and sustainable in their outcome. Overall, research shows that the regime against the pollution from oil-tankers was successful because it reached the intended aim to protect the seas from too much oil-discharge. Although one has to admit that this statement is only according to some bounded sources, the amount of accidentally spilt oil decreased significantly over the last 30 years.[98]

This, however, leads to the 'Why?' which seems to be somewhat easy to answer. The success of the regime is a mixture of technical advances, economic needs and political will. Load-on-top, the segregation of the ballast tanks and crude oil washing made fewer oil-discharges possible. In company with changes in international and national legislation these techniques helped to save much intentional releases.

---

[94] N.N. (1999)
[95] Frey (1993)
[96] Fichtner (2003) – Although technology is more modern, the ship will have still only one hull.
[97] N.N. (1999)
[98] ITOPF (n.a.)

Also the improvements of waste facilities and the expansion of services offered by harbours in accordance with the International Maritime Organisation were helpful for the environment.[99] Moreover a more efficient use of the oil aboard as well as an ever growing concern of the oil-owners about the waste of oil (e.g. with crude-oil-washing) led to the reduction of intentional oil-discharges. In addition to them the phase-in (at least scheduled) for double-hulls rather than single-hull-tankers is seen to have a beneficial influence on the amount of oil split accidentally as well.

For Greenpeace et al, however, these measures are not enough. They demand in addition to the mentioned changes a Global Maritime Distress and Safety System with a black-box known from airplanes. Within this relevant data is collected and in case of an accident sent to the harbour administration right away.[100]

Another way to force ship-owners to comply more with environmentally wishful developments outside or faster than the MARPOL 73/78 or the 1990 Oil-pollution Act would be the European-style rebate-system.[101] Countries like The Netherlands (Green Award) and Sweden have introduced lucrative systems that reduce the harbour fees significantly if a ship meets certain environmental standards.[102] In comparison, if a ship is worse than the average the crew will have to pay more. In general this idea seams to become successful if only more harbours and countries would join. Therefore at least an EU-wide phase-in could make sense.

Also the International Maritime Organisation itself urges improvements and suggests working more on a safety culture[103] on both, the side of flag states that have the ships registered as well as on the one of port states that get the ships.[104] The experts there also would like to see a concept of a safer culture with improved seafarers and management standards. Both, again, erects from the Safety Management Code and the Standards of Training Certificate.

Regardless the ideas for beyond, studies prove the impact of the International Maritime Organisation and the existing MARPOL 73/78 amongst others on the maritime environment.[105]

---

[99] Carpenter (2005)
[100] Heumer (1999)
[101] Carpenter (2005)
[102] Sesin (2002)
[103] IMO (1996) – p8 "need for a safety culture"
[104] IMO (1998a) – pp31
[105] Nelson (n.a.)

Without this the output of intentionally and unintentionally discharged oil might not have de-creased, but dramatically increased.[106] Therefore MARPOL 73/78 is today seen as the most important set of regulations[107] protecting the maritime life and limiting pollution at sea.[108]

---

[106] IMO (1996) – p7
[107] Huijer (n.a.)
[108] IMO (1998a) – pp31

5   Conclusion

Major spillages as well as steady oil-pollution have profound impacts on the maritime – and human – life. International regulations and conventions were formulated to address these issues. They have been put into practise and do now force ship-owners to cooperate with other national and international actors such as port authorities and their governments, shipyards and insurances. As of today, one can state that the measures taken have been successful as instruments on a global scale to prevent or at least reduce oil-pollution at sea because of their sense and need.[109]

The international regime did successfully regulate and eventually minimise the ship-generated oil-pollution by both, effective technical and political measures. As argued the MARPOL 73/78 equipment standards simplify the task of monitoring compared to discharging standards greatly. For the global public it obviously is easier to supervise just few big players than thousands of tankers globally. Moreover the costs of this regime were in an economical sense quite low. Since it caused success (environment) and the additional cost to any litre of oil was little.

Statistics about intended and unintended oil-discharges assume the amount of oil spilt has strongly gone down; but no one knows exact figures since much is only based on assumptions.[110] Trends, however, could be largely accounted to measures taken by the International Maritime Organisation (MARPOL 73 / 78, Convention for the Safety of Life at Sea 1974), national legislation (US Oil-pollution Act 1990) and concerns of ship-owners and their customers about financial liabilities.

These measures make the supply of oil and fuel to the final customer more expansive. But compared to the damage earlier discharging behaviour and accidents had on the environment this, however, is the better way to go.[111] Therefore the international community might be glad to have agreed on such treaties like MARPOL 73/78. However, although there is criticism

---

[109] Not to mention, however, some of the few cases in which ship-crews and senior seafarer have been found guilty of illegally discharging oil via secret hoses or fraudulent entries into the ship's board books.
[110] Peet (1994) – p44; MARPOL 73 / 78 has been credited for the decrease from 1970s to 1980s.

[111] N.N. (1990b)

since the agreement is not perfect, it seems to be far better for the future generations to have it than not to have it.